MW00876162

Winnie-the-Pooh's Picnic Cookbook

Inspired by **A. A. MILNE**

Winnie-the-Pooh's
PICNIC COOKBOOK

With Decorations by **ERNEST H. SHEPARD**

DUTTON BOOKS • NEW YORK

Library of Congress Cataloging-in-Publication Data
Winnie-the-Pooh's picnic cookbook / inspired by A. A. Milne;
with decorations by Ernest H. Shepard.   p.   cm.   Includes index.
ISBN 0-525-45533-7 (hardcover)   1. Cookery—Juvenile literature.
2. Picnicking—Juvenile literature.   3. Menus.   I. Milne, A. A.
(Alan Alexander), 1882–1956.   II. Shepard, Ernest H. (Ernest Howard),
1879–1976.   TX823.W56 1997   641.5'78—dc21   96-47814   CIP

Published in the United States 1997 by Dutton Children's Books,
a division of Penguin Books USA Inc.
375 Hudson Street, New York, New York 10014
Printed in Mexico
Written by Dawn Martin
Designed by Adrian Leichter
10 9 8 7 6 5 4 3 2 1

Contents

A Word About Picnics

It was a drowsy summer afternoon, and the Forest was full of gentle sounds . . .
—THE HOUSE AT POOH CORNER

Whether it's on a table under the boughs of Owl's shady tree, or a blanket on the floor of Rabbit's burrow, a picnic means fun, thanks to the magical combination of friends and family and food.

The following collection includes recipes for six picnics, with each menu serving about six people. The recipes can be divided or multiplied as your Picnic Needs Require, and simplified by the substitution of prepared sauces, dips, and dressings. Unless otherwise specified, use **large** eggs, **all-purpose** flour, **unsalted** butter, and **granulated** sugar. For best results, and for ease in blending, butter and eggs should be brought to room temperature before mixing.

Young cooks may need adult help with most of the recipes, particularly those that require the use of sharp utensils and the stove or oven. But no matter which picnic you pack, be sure to include a Little Something Extra. You never know when unexpected friends-and-relations might stop by.

• *Sandwich Safety*

To ensure that sandwiches and other perishables taste as good as they look—and develop no harmful bacteria—do not allow them to sit at room temperature for more than four hours. If you're planning a day trip, or have unexpected leftovers, use insulated coolers or thermal bags with freezer packs. Cakes, cookies, nuts, and popcorn can be stored safely at room temperature.

• *Picnic Protocol*

Picnics are about sharing—good times as well as good food—so it's important to leave your picnic area as clean, *if not cleaner,* than you found it. Dispose of garbage responsibly, and take home all the supplies that you brought. This way other picnickers can enjoy the spot as much as you did.

• *Sensible Supplies*

- Plates
- Cups
- Forks, knives, and spoons
- Napkins
- Serving utensils
- Sealed containers
- Premoistened towelettes
- Blankets

- Insect repellent
- Garbage bags

• *Extra-Special Expotitions*

Extra-special expotitions require extra-special supplies. Musical instruments, such as guitars (if anyone can play) or games (that everyone can play) add a Special Something to a picnic. And a book of poetry or a volume of *Winnie-the-Pooh* is wonderful for reading aloud. But for those who enjoy doing Nothing best, simply bring your imagination and find a Thoughtful Spot, and the rest will take care of itself.

Expotition Picnic

In a little while they were all ready at the top of the Forest, and the Expotition started. First came Christopher Robin and Rabbit, then Piglet and Pooh; then Kanga, with Roo in her pocket, and Owl; then Eeyore; and, at the end, in a long line, all Rabbit's friends-and-relations.

—Winnie-the-Pooh

∽ MENU ∽

Serves 6

Bug Juice

Roast Beef Sandwiches
WITH Horseradish OR Honey-Mustard Sauce

Baby Carrots AND Celery Sticks
WITH Cucumber Sour Cream Dip

Sugared Nuts

Chocolate-Chip Peanut-Butter Cookies

Extra supplies:
Binoculars for bird-watching

~ Bug Juice ~

1 *quart prepared fruit
  punch*
1 *quart ginger ale*
juice of one lemon
1 *jar of maraschino cherries*

Combine fruit punch, ginger ale, and lemon juice. Chill well. Stir in maraschino cherries.
Makes approximately 2 quarts.

6 *kaiser rolls*
horseradish sauce or
  honey-mustard sauce (see
  recipes on the next page)
1 *pound sliced roast beef*
2 *sliced tomatoes*

To assemble sandwiches, cut each roll and spread with horseradish or honey-mustard sauce. Arrange roast beef slices on bottom half of roll. Place 2 tomato slices on roast beef. Cover with top of kaiser roll.
Makes 6 sandwiches.

∾ Horseradish Sauce ∾

1 tablespoon drained
  prepared horseradish
1/2 cup sour cream

Combine ingredients in a small bowl. Mix
well. *Makes 1/2 cup.*

∾ Honey-Mustard Sauce ∾

1/4 cup Dijon mustard
1 teaspoon dry mustard
3 tablespoons honey
2 tablespoons white wine
  vinegar
1/2 cup peanut or canola oil

In a small bowl, combine mustard, dry mustard, honey, and vinegar. Slowly add oil,
whisking until mixture is thick. *Makes about
1/2 cup.*

·· Baby Carrots & Celery Sticks ··
with Cucumber Sour Cream Dip

BABY CARROTS & CELERY STICKS:

1 *pound baby carrots*
6 *celery stalks*

Bring water to a boil in a medium saucepan. Blanch carrots for about 3 minutes. Drain and rinse under cold water.

Rinse celery stalks, and cut into thirds. Slice each section into three sticks.

CUCUMBER SOUR CREAM DIP:

1 *large cucumber*
1 *pint sour cream*
*¹/₄ cup chopped chives
    and parsley*
*salt and freshly ground
    black pepper to taste*

Peel cucumber and remove seeds. Grate cucumber or mince well. Place cucumber in a strainer and squeeze out excess liquid.

In a small bowl, combine cucumber, sour cream, chives, and parsley. Mix well; add salt and pepper to taste. Keep refrigerated until ready to use. *Makes 1 pint.*

❧ Sugared Nuts ❧

2 1/2 cups mixed nuts,
  such as pecans, almonds,
  and peanuts
1 tablespoon cinnamon
1/4 teaspoon ginger
1/4 teaspoon nutmeg
2 tablespoons vegetable oil
1/2 cup sugar
1/2 teaspoon salt

Preheat oven to 350° F. Place mixed nuts in a small bowl. Heat cinnamon, ginger, and nutmeg in a pan over low heat until aromatic (about 15 seconds), then add oil. Stir until warm. Pour mixture over nuts, then toss with sugar and salt until evenly coated. Transfer nuts to foil-covered baking pan and bake 20 minutes, stirring occasionally, until nuts are toasted. *Makes approximately 2 1/2 cups.*

~ Chocolate-Chip ~
Peanut-Butter Cookies

1 cup softened butter
  (2 sticks)
1 cup sugar
¼ cup light brown sugar
1 egg
½ teaspoon baking soda
½ cup peanut butter
1 ½ cups flour
½ cup chocolate chips

Preheat oven to 350° F. Cream butter with both sugars until mixture is light and fluffy. Stir in egg, baking soda, and peanut butter. Add flour, and beat on medium speed until mixture is well blended. Stir in chocolate chips.

Drop rounded teaspoons of dough onto greased cookie sheet, leaving 2 inches between each cookie. Flatten cookies to ¼-inch thickness, using the bottom of a glass that has been sprayed with nonstick cooking spray or covered with waxed paper. Bake 7 to 9 minutes, or until edges begin to brown. Allow cookies to cool on cookie sheet for 2 minutes, then place them on wire racks and allow to cool completely. *Makes approximately 4 dozen cookies.*

Tea Party Picnic

Christopher Robin was at home by this time, because it was the afternoon, and he was so glad to see them that they stayed there until very nearly tea-time, and then they had a Very Nearly tea, which is one you forget about afterwards, and hurried on to Pooh Corner, so as to see Eeyore before it was too late to have a Proper Tea with Owl.
—THE HOUSE AT POOH CORNER

❧ **M E N U** ❧

Serves 6

Honey-Spiced Tea Punch

Blueberry Heart Scones WITH Smoked Turkey

Mini Orange-Pecan Muffins WITH Black Forest Ham

Cranberry-Orange Conserve

Waldorf Chicken Salad Sandwiches

Almond Shortbread Rounds

Raisin Spiced Tea Cake

Extra supplies:
Cloth napkins and fresh flowers

6 tea bags or 6 teaspoons
   of black tea, such as
   Earl Grey or Darjeeling
6 cups boiling water
juice of 2 lemons
juice of 2 oranges
1 cup unsweetened pineapple
   juice
2/3 cup sugar
1/2 cup honey
2 cups cold water
· 1 teaspoon whole cloves
1 cinnamon stick

Place tea bags or loose tea in a large saucepan and add boiling water. Steep 3 minutes, then strain and combine with fruit juices. In a separate pan, combine sugar, honey, cold water, cloves, and cinnamon stick and bring to a simmer. Add the tea mixture and simmer an additional 5 minutes. Chill, then garnish with sliced lemons and oranges. *Makes 2 quarts.*

∽ Blueberry Heart Scones ∽
with Smoked Turkey

2 cups flour
1/2 teaspoon salt
1/4 teaspoon baking soda
2 teaspoons baking powder
1/4 cup cold butter (1/2 stick),
    cut into small pieces
3/4 cup buttermilk
2 tablespoons molasses
1/2 cup blueberries
1/4 cup heavy cream (optional)
1 cup cranberry-orange
    conserve (optional; see
    recipe on page 23)
1/2 pound thinly sliced
    smoked turkey

Preheat oven to 400° F. In a large bowl, sift together flour, salt, baking soda, and baking powder. Using pastry cutter or hands, cut butter into mixture until crumbly. Stir in buttermilk and molasses. Add blueberries. Knead dough together on floured surface, pat dough into 1/2-inch-thick disk. Using a 2-inch heart-shaped cookie cutter, cut out as many hearts as possible. Transfer hearts to baking sheet lined with parchment paper, and brush tops with cream. Bake 10 minutes, or until the tops are a pale golden brown. Cool on rack.

To assemble, split scones and, if desired, spread with cranberry-orange conserve. Add 2 small squares of turkey to make a sandwich. *Makes approximately 20 tea sandwiches.*

～ Mini Orange-Pecan Muffins ～
with Black Forest Ham

1/2 cup softened butter
(1 stick)
1 cup sugar
2 large eggs
2 cups flour
1 teaspoon baking soda
1/3 teaspoon salt
1 cup buttermilk
1/3 cup sour cream
1 teaspoon orange extract
1 cup chopped raisins
1/2 cup chopped pecans
1 cup cranberry-orange
conserve (optional)
1/2 pound sliced Black Forest
ham

Preheat oven to 375° F. Spray mini-muffin pans with nonstick cooking spray. Cream butter and sugar. Stir in eggs. In a separate bowl, sift flour, baking soda, and salt together and stir into butter mixture. Stir in buttermilk, sour cream, and orange extract. Finally, stir in chopped raisins and pecans.

Spoon batter into muffin tins and bake 10 to 12 minutes, or until muffins are golden brown. Cool on racks.

To assemble, split muffins and spread with cranberry-orange conserve, if desired. Place a few small squares of ham inside each muffin to make a sandwich. *Makes approximately 30 tea sandwiches.*

zest of 2 oranges
²/₃ cup sugar
1 cup fresh orange juice
¹/₄ teaspoon ground ginger
¹/₄ teaspoon ground
   cinnamon
2 cups fresh or frozen
   cranberries

In a medium saucepan, combine orange zest, sugar, orange juice, ginger, and cinnamon, and bring to a boil. Reduce heat and simmer, stirring occasionally, for 10 minutes.

Add cranberries and cook until berries are tender (about 15 minutes). Remove from heat and allow to cool, stirring occasionally. Mixture will thicken as it cools. *Makes 2 cups.*

~ Waldorf Chicken ~ Salad Sandwiches

8 skinless and boneless
   chicken breasts
4 tablespoons butter
2 Granny Smith apples,
   peeled, cored, and diced
6 stalks of celery, diced
1 cup coarsely chopped
   walnuts
1 ½ cups mayonnaise
1 tablespoon orange zest
⅓ cup fresh orange juice
16 pieces of sandwich bread

Preheat oven to 350° F. Place chicken breasts and butter in a baking pan, cover, and bake until chicken is cooked (about 30 minutes). Cool and dice into ½-inch pieces. In a large bowl, combine chicken, apples, celery, and chopped nuts. In a separate bowl, whisk mayonnaise, orange zest, and orange juice together. Add to chicken mixture and toss well.

To assemble, spoon chicken salad onto a slice of bread, and top with a second slice. Cut each sandwich into quarters. *Makes 8 sandwiches.*

~ Almond Shortbread Rounds ~

1 cup flour
2 1/2 tablespoons cornstarch
pinch of salt
1/2 cup softened butter
    (1 stick)
1/2 cup sugar
1 1/2 teaspoons vanilla extract
1/2 cup finely chopped
    almonds

Preheat oven to 350° F. Sift together flour, cornstarch, and salt. In a separate bowl, cream butter, sugar, and vanilla extract until fluffy. Stir in flour mixture. Mix in nuts, using hands to stir, if necessary. Flatten dough between 2 sheets of waxed paper, and roll to 1/4-inch thickness. Remove top sheet of waxed paper.

Using a 3-inch round cookie cutter, cut out as many cookies as possible. Gather scraps together and repeat. Transfer cookies to ungreased cookie sheet, and bake for 10 to 12 minutes, or until cookies are a pale golden color. Remove from oven. Cool on sheet for 3 minutes and then transfer to racks and cool completely. *Makes approximately 16 cookies.*

✂ Raisin Spiced Tea Cake ✂

1 1/2 cups unbleached flour
1 teaspoon cinnamon
1 teaspoon ground ginger
1/2 teaspoon baking soda
3/4 cup softened butter
   (1 1/2 sticks)
1 cup sugar
3 eggs
1/4 cup fresh lemon juice
1/2 teaspoon lemon extract
1 cup golden raisins
1 tablespoon chopped
   crystallized ginger
confectioners' sugar
   for dusting

Preheat oven to 350° F. Grease and lightly flour a 7-cup tube pan. In a medium bowl, sift together flour, cinnamon, ginger, and baking soda. Set aside. Cream butter and granulated sugar until fluffy. Slowly add eggs, beating well after each addition. Stir in lemon juice, lemon extract, and flour mixture. Mix until well combined. Finally, stir in raisins and crystallized ginger.

Pour into prepared pan and bake for 50 minutes, or until toothpick inserted in center of cake comes out clean. Cool cake in pan for 20 minutes, then invert onto rack and cool completely. Dust with confectioners' sugar.

Birthday Party Picnic

"Eeyore," said Owl, "Christopher Robin is giving a party."
"Very interesting," said Eeyore. "I suppose they will be sending me down the odd bits which got trodden on."

—WINNIE-THE-POOH

·ᴄ M E N U ᴄ·

Serves 6

Very Berry Party Punch

Barbecued-Chicken Sandwiches

Spiral Pasta WITH Cherry Tomatoes AND Basil

Carrot Salad WITH Cinnamon AND Raisins

Chocolate Sour Cream Cake

Chocolate-Dipped Strawberries

·Extra supplies:
Birthday candles and party hats

⁓ Very Berry Party Punch ⁓

2 pounds frozen strawberries,
  thawed
1 1/2 cups superfine sugar
4 cups cold water or
  seltzer water
2 cups unsweetened pineapple
  juice
juice of 2 lemons
6–8 fresh strawberries
  (optional)

In a large bowl, mix together strawberries and their syrup and sugar. Puree in blender, and strain through a fine mesh strainer. Combine with water. Add pineapple and lemon juice. If desired, garnish with fresh strawberries. *Makes 2 quarts.*

·~ Barbecued-Chicken Sandwiches ·~

2/3 cup ketchup
1/2 cup unsulfured molasses
1/3 cup yellow mustard
2 tablespoons cider vinegar
2 teaspoons Worcestershire
   sauce
1 teaspoon soy sauce
6 skinless and boneless
   chicken breasts
6 kaiser rolls

In a large bowl, whisk ketchup, molasses, mustard, vinegar, Worcestershire sauce, and soy sauce. Reserve 1/2 cup of sauce mixture, and pour the rest over the chicken breasts. Marinate for 30 minutes.

Grill or broil chicken for about 10 minutes, or until chicken is cooked through.

To assemble, slice chicken on the diagonal and arrange on bottom half of sliced roll. Spoon sauce over chicken, and cover with top of roll. *Makes 6 sandwiches.*

❧ Spiral Pasta with ❧ Cherry Tomatoes & Basil

3 cups cherry tomatoes
1/2 cup olive oil
1/2 teaspoon crushed red
    pepper flakes (optional)
1/2 teaspoon salt
1 pound fusilli pasta
1/2 cup fresh chopped
    basil leaves
1 cup Parmesan cheese,
    grated

Slice cherry tomatoes into quarters. In a small bowl, combine tomatoes, olive oil, red pepper flakes, and salt. Marinate for 30 minutes.

Bring a large pot of water to a boil and cook fusilli for 10 to 13 minutes, or until desired tenderness. Drain and reserve 1/3 cup of pasta water. Add the warm water to the tomatoes and toss well. Combine pasta and tomatoes and toss with basil. Add the Parmesan cheese and toss again.

❧ Carrot Salad with ❧ Cinnamon & Raisins

¹/₂ cup raisins
¹/₄ cup cider vinegar
salt and freshly ground
    black pepper to taste
¹/₄ teaspoon cinnamon
¹/₂ cup light olive oil
1 ¹/₂ pounds grated carrots

Soak raisins in vinegar for 20 minutes. Drain and reserve vinegar. In a separate bowl, whisk vinegar, salt, pepper, and cinnamon together. Slowly add oil, whisking until combined. In a medium bowl, combine raisins and carrots. Pour vinegar mixture over carrot mixture and toss well.

~ Chocolate Sour Cream Cake ~

2 ounces semisweet chocolate
1 cup softened butter
  (2 sticks)
2 cups sugar
3 large eggs
1 teaspoon vanilla extract
1 1/2 cups all-purpose flour
1/2 cup cocoa powder
1/4 teaspoon salt
1 cup sour cream

Preheat oven to 350° F. Spray a 9 x 5-inch loaf pan with nonstick cooking spray. Set aside.

Chop chocolate into small pieces, and melt in a double boiler or a small pan set over simmering water. Remove from heat and cool.

Cream butter and sugar until fluffy. Slowly add eggs, beating well after each addition. Stir in vanilla extract and cooled chocolate. Sift flour, cocoa, and salt together. Fold half of flour mixture into butter mixture. Fold in 1/2 cup of sour cream. Fold in remaining flour mixture, and then remaining sour cream. Stir until all ingredients are incorporated.

Pour into prepared pan and bake for 1 hour, or until toothpick inserted in center of cake comes out clean. Cool in pan. *Makes one 9 x 5-inch cake.*

✒ Chocolate-Dipped Strawberries ✒

3 *ounces bittersweet chocolate*
1 *tablespoon butter*
1 *teaspoon vanilla or orange*
  extract
12 *large strawberries*

Chop chocolate into small pieces. In a double boiler combine chocolate, butter, and vanilla or orange extract. Stir until chocolate is melted and smooth. Remove from heat.

Dip strawberries halfway into chocolate and place on waxed paper. Refrigerate until chocolate has set, about 10 minutes. Store in a cool place. *Makes 12.*

Rainy Day Picnic

"The atmospheric conditions have been very unfavourable lately," said Owl.
"The what?"
"It has been raining," explained Owl.
"Yes," said Christopher Robin. *"It has."*

—Winnie-the-Pooh

~ **M E N U** ~
Serves 6

Mulled Cider

Pecan Chicken Fingers

Red-Potato Salad

Spinach Salad WITH Balsamic-Vinegar Dressing

Buttermilk Biscuits

Almond-Cream Fingers

Peach Cobbler

Extra supplies:
A blanket to spread on the living-room floor
and board games to play after lunch

∾ Mulled Cider ∾

2 quarts apple cider
4 cinnamon sticks
2 apples, studded with cloves
5 whole allspice

Combine ingredients in a large saucepan and simmer for 30 minutes. Strain and serve warm. *Makes 2 quarts.*

❧ Pecan Chicken Fingers ❧

6 *skinless and boneless*
  chicken breasts
2 *cups coarsely ground pecans*
1 *cup flour*
1 *teaspoon salt*
1 ½ *cups maple syrup*
1 *cup canola oil*

Place chicken between waxed paper and flatten slightly with a meat pounder. Cut each breast into 4 strips. Mix ground pecans, flour, and salt together in a small bowl. Pour maple syrup into a separate small bowl and dip each chicken strip into the maple syrup. Then roll each strip in the pecan-flour mixture.

Heat oil, and sauté chicken until brown (about 3 minutes each side).

⤳ Red-Potato Salad ⤳

2 pounds small red potatoes
3 tablespoons dry white wine
　(optional)
2 teaspoons chopped fresh dill
1 1/2 tablespoons red wine
　vinegar
3 tablespoons Dijon mustard
1/2 teaspoon salt
1/3 cup light olive oil
freshly ground black pepper
　to taste
2 tablespoons chopped
　scallions

Place potatoes in a medium saucepan with water and bring to a boil. Reduce heat to medium and cook until potatoes are tender (about 15 minutes). Drain and cut potatoes into quarters. Sprinkle with white wine and fresh dill. Set aside.

In a separate bowl, whisk together vinegar, mustard, and salt. Slowly add olive oil, whisking until all ingredients are combined. Pour over potatoes and toss well. Add pepper to taste. Sprinkle scallions on top.

~ Spinach Salad with ~ Balsamic-Vinegar Dressing

3 to 4 bunches small-leafed
    spinach

DRESSING:
1/4 cup balsamic vinegar
1 tablespoon Dijon mustard
2/3 to 3/4 cup olive oil
salt and freshly ground
    black pepper to taste

1 ripe pear

Remove stems from spinach, wash, and pat or spin-dry. Place in a plastic bag, and refrigerate until ready to serve.

Pour vinegar into a small bowl and whisk in mustard. Slowly add oil while whisking vigorously. Season with salt and pepper.

To serve: peel, core, and slice pear. Combine with spinach in a medium-sized bowl. Add salad dressing and toss well. Serve immediately.

~ Buttermilk Biscuits ~

1 1/2 *cups unbleached flour*
1 1/2 *teaspoons baking powder*
3/4 *teaspoon salt*
1/2 *teaspoon baking soda*
1/2 *teaspoon sugar*
6 *tablespoons cold unsalted butter, cut into small pieces*
1/2 *cup buttermilk*

Preheat oven to 400° F. In a medium bowl, sift together flour, baking powder, salt, baking soda, and sugar. Using a pastry cutter or fingers, cut butter into flour mixture until mixture is crumbly. Stir in buttermilk.

On a lightly floured surface, knead dough until it is smooth (about six times). Pat dough into a rectangle of about 1-inch thickness and cut into 8 2-inch squares. Or use a 2-inch biscuit cutter and cut 8 rounds. Shape any excess dough into an additional biscuit. Bake on ungreased baking sheet until biscuits are golden brown (about 15 minutes). *Makes 8 biscuits.*

~ Almond-Cream Fingers ~

1 cup flour
1/4 cup sugar
6 tablespoons softened butter
2 tablespoons finely chopped
   almonds
1 tablespoon molasses
1/2 teaspoon baking powder
2 tablespoons heavy cream
3 tablespoons confectioners'
   sugar

Preheat oven to 400° F. Combine all ingredients in a small bowl, and mix with a wooden spoon (or with the hands, if necessary). Mix until all ingredients are thoroughly combined into a dough. Chill for 1 hour.

Roll dough into finger-sized logs. Bake on greased cookie sheets for 10 to 12 minutes, or until cookies are a pale golden brown. While warm, roll cookies in confectioners' sugar. *Makes 2 dozen cookies.*

❧ Peach Cobbler ❧

2 tablespoons cornstarch
$1/2$ cup water
$1/3$ cup dark brown sugar
6 cups sliced peaches
1 tablespoon butter
1 tablespoon lemon juice

TOPPING:
1 cup flour
1 tablespoon sugar
$1 1/2$ teaspoons baking
    powder
$1/4$ cup softened butter
    ($1/2$ stick)
1 egg
$1/2$ cup milk
$1/2$ cup sour cream

Preheat oven to 400° F. In a medium saucepan combine cornstarch and water, and stir until cornstarch is dissolved. Add brown sugar and peaches and cook over low heat until the mixture thickens (about 8 to 10 minutes). Remove from heat, and stir in butter and lemon juice. Pour mixture into an 8-inch-square baking dish.

In a medium bowl, mix flour, sugar, and baking powder. Using a pastry cutter, cut in butter until mixture is crumbly. Set aside.

In a small bowl, beat egg, and combine with milk and sour cream. Stir into flour mixture.

Pour topping over the peaches and bake for 25 minutes. Cobbler should be golden brown.

Kids' Picnic

One day when the sun had come back over the Forest, bringing with it the scent of May . . . Christopher Robin whistled in a special way he had, and Owl came flying out of the Hundred Acre Wood . . .

—WINNIE-THE-POOH

∾ **M E N U** ∾
Serves 6

Pink Lemonade WITH Strawberries

Peanut Butter, Apple & Bacon Sandwiches

Cherry Tomatoes
WITH Clover-Honey Dressing

Ambrosia Fruit Salad

Caramel-Nut Popcorn

Candy Cookies

Extra supplies:
A kite

∿ Pink Lemonade ∿
with Strawberries

½ pint strawberries
1 ½ cups superfine sugar
juice of 10 large lemons
2 quarts cold water

Slice strawberries and sprinkle with ½ cup sugar. Allow to stand for 30 minutes. Combine lemon juice and cold water. Stir in remaining cup of sugar. Add strawberries and their syrup and stir well. *Makes about 2 quarts.*

Peanut Butter, Apple & Bacon Sandwiches

18 slices of bacon
12 slices of bread
1 1/2 cups peanut butter
3 crisp apples
1 cup alfalfa sprouts
   (optional)

Fry bacon until crisp, and drain on paper towels. Lightly toast bread and spread with peanut butter. Core and slice apples. Layer bacon (three strips per sandwich), apple, and alfalfa sprouts on bottom half of sandwich. Top with remaining bread and cut into quarters. *Makes 6 sandwiches.*

∽ Cherry Tomatoes with ∽ Clover-Honey Dressing

2 pounds cherry tomatoes

DRESSING:
*1/4 cup balsamic or white
    wine vinegar*
3 tablespoons clover honey
3/4 cup light olive oil
salt to taste

GARNISH:
*2 tablespoons chopped
    fresh basil*
*2 tablespoons chopped fresh
    flat-leaf parsley*

Slice tomatoes in half and place in a small bowl. Set aside.

In another small bowl, combine vinegar and honey. Slowly add oil, whisking vigorously. Salt to taste. Drizzle honey dressing over top of tomatoes. Sprinkle with basil and parsley.

~ Ambrosia Fruit Salad ~

3 seedless oranges
1 pint strawberries
1/2 pound seedless green
   grapes
1/2 pound seedless red grapes
1/2 cup mini marshmallows

Peel and section oranges. Hull and slice strawberries. Remove grapes from stems. In a medium bowl, combine fruit and marshmallows.

~ Caramel-Nut Popcorn ~

3 quarts freshly popped
  popcorn (about 1/2 cup
  unpopped corn)
2 cups roasted unsalted
  peanuts
1 cup dark brown sugar
1/2 cup light corn syrup
1/2 cup butter (1 stick)
1/2 teaspoon salt
2 teaspoons vanilla extract
1/2 teaspoon baking soda

Preheat oven to 250° F. Grease a large roasting pan and place popcorn and nuts inside. In a heavy saucepan combine brown sugar, corn syrup, butter, and salt. Place over medium heat and stir constantly. Bring to a boil. Boil for about 4 minutes, then remove from stove. Stir in vanilla extract and baking soda. Pour glaze over popcorn and stir well.

Bake popcorn for about 1 hour. Use metal spatula to loosen popcorn from bottom of pan. Allow mixture to cool, then break into bite-sized clumps.

⁖ Candy Cookies ⁖

1 cup softened butter
   (2 sticks)
1 cup light brown sugar
1/2 cup sugar
2 eggs
1 teaspoon vanilla extract
2 1/4 cups all-purpose flour
1/4 teaspoon salt
1 teaspoon baking soda
1 cup M&M's candies

Preheat oven to 375° F. Cream butter and both sugars until fluffy. Mix in eggs and vanilla extract. In a separate bowl, sift flour, salt, and baking soda together. Add flour mixture to butter and beat well. Stir in candy.

Drop rounded teaspoons of batter onto ungreased cookie sheet. Bake for 10 to 12 minutes, or until cookies are golden brown. Allow to cool on cookie sheets for 2 minutes, then transfer to racks and cool further. *Makes 3 dozen cookies.*

Beach Picnic

We had sand in the eyes and the ears and
    the nose,
And sand in the hair, and sand-between-
    the-toes.
Whenever a good nor' wester blows,
Christopher is certain of
Sand-between-the-toes.

          —WHEN WE WERE VERY YOUNG

❧ **MENU** ❧

Serves 6

Pineapple-Kiwi Cooler

Crab Salad Sandwiches WITH Tomatoes AND Avocado
IN Homemade Pita Bread

Grilled Shrimp WITH Garlic

Spicy Corn & Tomato Salad

Green Beans WITH Ginger-Honey Dressing

Bittersweet-Chocolate Chunk Brownies

Extra supplies:
Beach umbrellas and sunscreen

∾ Pineapple-Kiwi Cooler ∾

4 cups unsweetened pineapple
    juice
4 kiwis, peeled and sliced
juice of 3 lemons
 ¹/₂ cup cream of coconut
4 cups crushed ice

Working with one quarter of each ingredient
at a time, blend them in an electric blender
until creamy. Chill before serving. *Makes
approximately 2 quarts.*

⁓ Crab Salad Sandwiches ⁓
with Tomatoes & Avocado

3 tablespoons lemon juice
1 tablespoon Dijon mustard
1/2 cup mayonnaise
2/3 cup finely chopped celery
2 tablespoons chopped parsley
1 cup chopped scallions
1 pound lump crabmeat
1/2 teaspoon salt
freshly ground black pepper
    to taste
1/2 teaspoon cayenne pepper
    (optional)
8 homemade pitas (see recipe
    on next page)
2 sliced tomatoes
1 sliced avocado

In a large bowl, combine lemon juice, mustard, and mayonnaise, and mix well. Stir in chopped celery, parsley, scallions, and crabmeat. Season with salt, pepper, and cayenne pepper. Keep crab salad chilled in a sealed container until just ready to serve. Sandwiches should be assembled just prior to eating.

To assemble, split pitas. Spoon crab mixture into pita, and add slices of tomato and avocado to each sandwich. *Makes 8 sandwiches.*

∾ Homemade Pita Bread ∾

1 1/4 cups warm water
1 teaspoon dry yeast
3 cups flour
1/2 tablespoon salt
1/2 tablespoon olive oil

Pour warm water into a large bowl and stir in yeast. Using an electric beater with a paddle attachment, slowly mix in 1½ cups flour. Cover bowl, and allow dough to sit in a warm spot until it has doubled in size (about 1½ hours).

Sprinkle salt over dough and add olive oil. Slowly add the remaining flour, and mix on low speed until dough is smooth.

Turn dough out of bowl, and knead 12 times. Oil bowl and replace dough. Cover and allow to rise again until dough doubles in size.

Preheat oven to 450° F. Cut dough in half. Cut each half into 4 pieces, and roll each into a ball. On a floured surface, roll out each ball into a circle that is about ¼ inch thick and 6 inches in diameter. Bake on ungreased baking sheet for 6 to 8 minutes, or until pitas are light brown and puffy. *Makes 8 pitas.*

ᛋ Grilled Shrimp with Garlic ᛋ

12 to 18 *large shrimp*
1/2 cup freshly squeezed lemon
   juice
1/2 cup olive oil
3 cloves garlic, crushed
2 teaspoons chopped parsley
1/2 teaspoon red pepper flakes
   (optional)
pinch each of salt and freshly
   ground black pepper

Peel, wash, and devein shrimp. Arrange in a shallow pan. In a medium bowl, combine remaining ingredients. Pour over shrimp and marinate in the refrigerator for 1 hour. Remove the shrimp from the marinade, and grill or broil until done (about 3 minutes per side).

~ Spicy Corn & Tomato Salad ~

2 cups water
2 cups fresh corn kernels
1 teaspoon salt
4 ripe tomatoes
1/2 cup finely minced sweet
    onion (such as Vidalia)
3 tablespoons minced cilantro
4 tablespoons minced flat-leaf
    parsley
4 tablespoons lemon juice
1/2 cup olive oil
1 1/2 teaspoons ground cumin
2 teaspoons chili powder
salt to taste

In a small saucepan, bring 2 cups of water to a boil. Add corn and salt, and cook until tender (about 2 minutes). Drain and transfer to a medium bowl. Blanch tomatoes in boiling water for 1 minute. Drain, peel, and remove seeds. Dice tomatoes and combine with corn. Add onion, cilantro, and parsley.

Pour lemon juice into a small bowl and slowly add olive oil, stirring well. Stir in cumin and chili powder and pour over tomatoes and corn. Toss well. Salt to taste.

~ Green Beans with ~ Ginger-Honey Dressing

2 pounds green beans

DRESSING:

1 teaspoon fresh ginger, peeled
  and finely chopped
1 clove garlic, finely minced
1/4 cup rice wine vinegar
2 tablespoons soy sauce
1 tablespoon honey
1/2 cup peanut or canola oil
1/4 teaspoon hot chili oil
  (optional)

Blanch beans in boiling water until tender (about 3 to 4 minutes). Drain and cool. Set aside.

Combine ginger, garlic, rice wine vinegar, soy sauce, and honey in a small bowl. Whisk well. Continue whisking, and slowly add oil. If desired, whisk in hot chili oil. Pour over beans and toss.

·⁘· Bittersweet-Chocolate ·⁘· Chunk Brownies

4 ounces unsweetened
   chocolate, chopped into
   small pieces
$1/2$ cup butter (1 stick)
$1 1/2$ cups sugar
1 teaspoon vanilla extract
$1/4$ teaspoon salt
3 eggs
$3/4$ cup flour
1 cup bittersweet chocolate,
   chopped into chunks

Preheat oven to 350° F. Butter and line an 8-inch-square baking pan with parchment paper.

In a small saucepan, combine unsweetened chocolate and butter, and stir over low heat until melted. Remove from heat and cool slightly.

Stir sugar, vanilla extract, and salt into butter mixture. Slowly add eggs, beating well after each addition. Stir in flour until blended. Stir in chocolate chunks. Pour batter into prepared pan and bake for 40 minutes. Cool in pan, then invert onto rack. Cut into 16 squares. *Makes 16 brownies.*

After they had walked a little way Christopher Robin said:

"What do you like doing best in the world, Pooh?"

"Well," said Pooh, "what I like best . . . is Me and Piglet going to see You, and You saying 'What about a little something?' and Me saying, 'Well, I shouldn't mind a little something, should you, Piglet,' and it being a hummy sort of day outside, and birds singing. . . ."

They walked on . . . and by-and-by they came to an enchanted place on the very top of the Forest . . . Sitting there they could see the whole world spread out until it reached the sky . . .
—THE HOUSE AT POOH CORNER

Index